SCHIRMER'S LIBRARY
OF MUSICAL CLASSICS

Vol. 2007

MODESTE MOUSSORGSKY

Pictures at an Exhibition

For Piano

ISBN 978-0-7935-3889-8

G. SCHIRMER, *Inc.*

DISTRIBUTED BY

HAL•LEONARD®
CORPORATION
7777 W. BLUEMOUND RD. P.O. BOX 13819 MILWAUKEE, WI 53213

Preface

Painter and architect Victor Hartmann, a close friend of Modeste Moussorgsky, died in August 1873. The following year an exhibition of his works was held. On a visit to the exhibition Moussorgsky was moved to compose musical illustrations to some of the drawings and watercolors. The resulting masterpiece was *Pictures at an Exhibition* for piano, a cycle of ten pieces with connecting interludes. Moussorgsky composed the entire work in about three weeks.

In spite of the great popularity this work has attained it seldom is performed in its original version. The work's first editors considered Moussorgsky's harsh harmonies too daring for the time and removed them. Though the editors meant well their modifications and additions altered Moussorgsky's highly original and astringent musical language. Later editors not only adopted these changes, but even added their own distortions.

This edition presents the work as Moussorgsky originally composed it.

Program

Page

Promenade   11

These interludes represent the composer at an exhibition of drawings by the painter Victor Hartmann, "moving now to the left, now to the right, now wandering about aimlessly, now eagerly making for one of the pictures. . . ."

1. **The Gnome** 12

A dwarf walks about awkwardly on crooked little legs.

Promenade   15

2. **The Old Castle** 16

A castle in the Middle Ages, in front of which stands a troubadour singing.

Promenade   20

3. **The Tuileries** 20

Subtitled *Children Quarrelling After Play* this depicts an avenue in the Tuileries gardens populated by a crowd of children and nurses.

4. **The Ox-Cart** 23

A Polish cart (Bydlo) with huge wheels that is drawn by oxen.

Promenade   25

5. **Ballet of the Chicks in their Shells** 26

This drawing illustrates a scene from the ballet "Trilby," in which newborn chickens dance as they leave their shells.

6. **Samuel Goldenberg and Schmuyle** 28

Two Polish Jews; one rich, the other poor.

Promenade   31

7. **The Market Place in Limoges** 32

French women haggle over goods in the market place.

8. **The Catacombs** 36

In this drawing Hartmann portrayed himself contemplating the interior of the Paris catacombs by the light of a lantern. The second part of this movement is an Andante in b minor that Moussorgsky titled *Con mortuis in lingua mortua*. This translates as "with the dead in the language of the dead." Above the original manuscript Moussorgsky wrote: "L'esprit créateur de Hartmann défunt me méne vers les crânes et les apostrophe—les crânes s'allument doucement à l'intérieur."

9. **The Hut on Fowl's Legs** 38

The drawing shows a clock in the shape of Baba Yaga's hut which, in Russian mythology, was said to have been built on chicken's claws so it could turn to meet each newcomer. Baba Yaga was a witch who lured lost souls to her hut and ate them.

10. **The Great Gate of Kiev** 46

This drawing is an architectural sketch for a magnificent Gate to the town of Kiev, done in the massive old Russian style and with a cupola shaped like a star helmet. The original manuscript reads *The Bohatyr-Gate of the Town of Kiev*. The Bohatyrs were mythological Russian heroes; princes who made Kiev the principal area for their occupation: hunting.

Cathedral Tower, Périgueux

Chick Costume for Trilbi

Clock in the Form of Baba-Yaga's Hut

The Great Gate of Kiev

PICTURES at an EXHIBITION

Modeste Moussorgsky
(1874)

Promenade

Allegro giusto, nel modo russico, senza allegrezza, ma poco sostenuto

1. The Gnome

Meno mosso

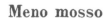

Poco a poco accelerando

Sempre vivo

Promenade

Moderato commodo assai e con delicatezza

2. The Old Castle

Andantino molto cantabile e con dolore

Promenade

Moderato non tanto, pesamente

3. The Tuileries

Allegretto non troppo, capriccioso

4. The Ox-Cart

Promenade

Tranquillo

5. Ballet of the Chicks in their Shells

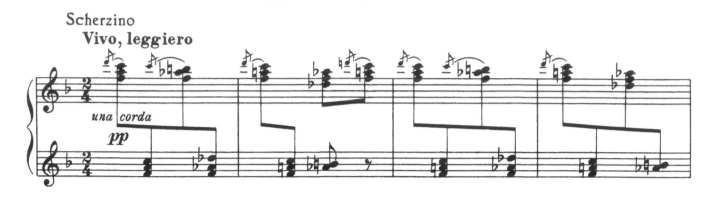

Trio

Da Capo il Scherzino, senza Trio,
e poi Coda

Coda

6. Samuel Goldenberg and Schmuyle

Andantino

Allegro giusto, nel modo russico, poco sostenuto

7. The Market Place in Limoges

Allegretto vivo, sempre scherzando

Meno mosso sempre capriccioso

poco accelerando

8. The Catacombs

Sepulcrum romanum

Con mortuis in lingua mortua

9. The Hut on Fowl's Legs

Allegro con brio, feroce

Andante mosso

Allegro molto

10. The Great Gate of Kiev

Allegro alla breve. Maestoso. Con grandezza

Meno mosso, sempre maestoso